Windup Train Repair

James Pekarek

ISBN: 1540583635
ISBN-13: 978-1540583635

CHRISTMAS 1972

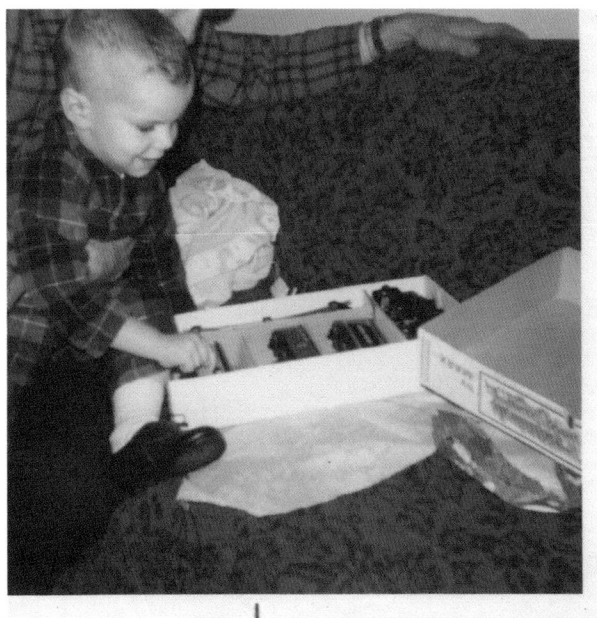

I open up my first train – a Marx Mechanical #526 set – while sitting on my Dad's lap.

CONTENTS

ACKNOWLEDGMENTS

Although this is a small book, it is the product of many years of learning about and working on windup trains. It would not be possible to write it without a lot of help over the years from my friends on the Yahoo Marx Train Group, the Windup-Toy-Trains-R-Us Facebook group, and the Marx Train Facebook group. My friends Al Osterud and Gary Anderson have forgotten more about Marx trains that I will ever know, and have always generously shared their knowledge with me. Steve Eastman and Walt Hiteshaw have also been helpful and supportive through the years. Kevin VonKluck graciously helped with proofreading, as did my wife Karin. Of course, my Dad has always been willing to tackle the difficult repairs of machinery that others could not or would not do...

PREFACE

Watching a vintage windup train running around a track is one of life's little pleasures. It is amazing that a toy train manufactured years, decades, or even a century ago can still operate just like the day it left the factory. Manufacturers such as Ives, Hafner, American Flyer and Marx made very reliable and long lasting O gauge windup mechanisms.

However, like any mechanical device, windup trains will sometimes develop problems. Unfortunately, there are very few people who are willing to attempt repairs on windup motors. There tends to be a certain mystery that surrounds the mechanisms. Combine that mystery with a lack of replacement parts, a motor that was never meant to be taken apart and a mainspring that is coiled up like a snake ready to strike, and those innocent little windup trains seem to have a Doctor Jekyll & Mr. Hyde personality.

It is my hope that this book will take some of the mystery out of windup train repair. There are a variety of techniques that can be used to work on the "unrepairable" motors. Some problems are simple and may be addressed with a minimum amount of tools and talent. Other issues are more complex, and may require machine tools and a certain level of skill in order to correct them. It is up to you – the reader – to assess your skill level and determine what repairs you are willing to tackle. Patience and practice will help you get your windup train running once again.

Let's repair some windup trains!

CHAPTER 1
WINDUP MOTOR DESIGN AND THEORY

In order to diagnose and repair windup train motors, it is necessary to have a basic understanding of how the mechanism works, as well as the functions of the various components. Fortunately, most windup motors are very similar in function and design with a few differences in the details of construction. We will get started with a few definitions to familiarize us with the various parts that make up a typical mechanism.

Mainspring: This is the largest spring in the motor, and it is used to store mechanical energy. In a typical windup train motor, this is a flat spring that is wound in a spiral shape. The mainspring is sometimes referred to as simply "the spring".

Ratchet: A device that disengages two parts when turned one direction, yet locks the same two parts together when turned in the opposite direction.

Mainspring Hub: A part that attaches to the inside end of the mainspring. It may be connected to a key to wind the spring, and/or may transfer power from the mainspring to the gears of the motor.

Sideplates: The large flat plates that make up the basic frame of the motor. They are usually located just inside of the drive wheels, and contain the mainspring and mechanism between them.

Crossmember: Frame parts that connect the two sideplates together. They may have a round or rectangular cross section.

Axle: A round shaft that is used to hold the flanged wheels in place. If it is used to transfer power to the wheels, it is a drive axle. If it is not driven, it is an idler axle.

Pinion Gear: A small gear, usually machined out of solid brass or steel.

Gearset: Two gears that are joined together, usually consisting of a pinion gear and a larger gear that may be either stamped out of sheet metal or machined from steel or brass.

Big Gear: Typically the largest gear in the motor, it is connected to the mainspring hub and may be part of the ratchet assembly.

Intermediate Shaft: A shaft that is located in between the mainspring hub and drive axle. There may be one or more intermediate shafts. Each one typically carries a gearset.

Governor: A device used to limit the operating speed of the motor.

Centrifugal Governor: A governor that consists of a spring loaded weight rotating within a stationary drum.

Escapement: A governor that consists of a toothed escape wheel (similar to a gear) driving an anchor that rocks back and forth.

Brake: A device used to keep the motor from running when the spring is wound up.

Theory of Operation

A windup motor operates on a simple premise. A key is used by the operator to store mechanical energy in the mainspring. The energy is released from the mainspring through the gears to the drive axle, which propels the motor down the track. A governor keeps the speed of the motor in check.

The actual operation and construction of a windup motor is a bit more complex. The mainspring is capable of delivering a relatively large amount of torque, but can only do it for a few revolutions. However, a toy train only needs a small amount of torque at the drive axle to move it down the track, but it should run for as long as possible which requires many revolutions of the drive wheels. In order to accomplish this, a series of gears is used to connect the mainspring to the drive axle. The gears allow a single revolution of the mainspring to spin the drive wheels multiple times. Conversely, the large torque of the mainspring is reduced by the same ratio to a useable level at the drive wheels.

In practical terms, the outside end of the mainspring is usually attached to a crossmember and the inside end of the mainspring is connected to the mainspring hub. The hub transmits the power from the mainspring to the big gear. The big gear meshes with a small pinion gear on the first intermediate shaft. The pinion gear is usually part of a gearset, so power is transferred from the pinion to a somewhat larger gear. The larger gear meshes with a pinion on the next intermediate shaft, or possibly on the drive axle depending on how the motor is designed.

In a typical motor, a key is connected directly to the mainspring hub for the purpose of winding up the mainspring, and a ratchet is used to disconnect the mainspring and hub from the rest of the mechanism. This makes it much easier to wind, since the operator only has to supply the energy needed to wind the spring without requiring additional energy to needlessly spin the rest of the mechanism. By holding the drive wheels either by hand or with a brake, the ratchet makes it very convenient to wind the motor. The key is normally rotated a half-turn at a time, then the operator has to let go of it to get another grasp on it to wind it another half-turn. When the operator lets go of the key, the ratchet reconnects the mainspring to the gears, and the brake (or hand) keeps the drive wheels from spinning and thus prevents the spring from unwinding. Hafner motors (including early AF motors designed by Hafner) use a different design where the outer end of the mainspring is connected to a basket that is rotated by the key for the purpose of winding up the motor; we will look at it in detail later in the book.

Since gears are used to increase the number of revolutions of the drive wheels compared to the mainspring, a windup motor is capable of reaching very high speeds. Some sort of governor is needed to limit the speed of the train. Most motors use some variation of a centrifugal governor, where a weight is attached to a shaft with a small governor spring to counter it. When the shaft spins up to speed, the centrifugal force on the weight overcomes the spring, and the weight moves away from the shaft. The assembly spins inside a stationary drum, so when the weight moves outward it comes in contact with the drum. The friction between the moving weight and stationary drum keeps the motor from speeding up any further. Should the motor slow down, there will be less centrifugal force acting on the weight and the governor spring will pull it away from the drum. This reduces or eliminates friction, and more power is delivered to the drive wheels.

Some manufacturers used a crude escapement instead of a centrifugal governor. The teeth on the escape wheel act on the pallets of an anchor, forcing the anchor to rock back and forth as the motor is running. When the motor reaches a certain speed, the force needed to make the anchor oscillate back and forth will become equal to the power that the mainspring is able to deliver, limiting the speed of the motor.

Now that we have a basic understanding of the operation and design of the windup motor, we can start examining the various parts in detail.

Marx Ratchet Motor Parts

1. Big Gear
2. Ratchet Assembly
3. 1st Intermediate Shaft and Gearset
4. 2nd Intermediate Shaft and Gearset
5. Drive axle and Gearset
6. Centrifugal Governor
7. Mainspring
8. Crossmember
9. Sparker Gearset
10. Sparking Wheel

This is a view of a Marx Ratchet Motor with the right sideplate removed. This particular motor has a sparking wheel which was located under the smoke stack. A flint (not shown) is held against the sparking wheel, generating sparks which then flew out of the smoke stack.

It isn't obvious from this angle, but the intermediate gearsets each have a small brass pinion gear that is located behind the stamped steel gears. A picture of a Marx intermediate gearset can be seen at the top of page 31.

Although it isn't noted in the list, the end of the mainspring hub can be seen in the middle of the big gear/ratchet assembly – it is the gray round part with a square hole in the middle. A better view of the ratchet assembly can be seen on page 41.

CHAPTER 2
CLEANING AND LUBRICATION

It is a simple fact: windup trains have a limited amount of power. In order to make the most of that power, the mechanism needs to run smoothly and with a minimum of drag. The first step to having a smooth running mechanism is to make sure it is clean and properly lubricated.

Motors may have a variety of contaminants in them; dirt, rust, congealed oils, even carpet fibers or pet hair. I like to look for fibers first. They are often wound up behind the wheels or in the gears and shafts. They can be removed with tweezers, although it may help to cut them out with a sharp knife. Next, I like to blow the motor out with compressed air to remove loose dirt and rust. If the motor is extremely rusty, it might be a good idea to soak it in a cleaner such as Evapo-Rust, although most can be flushed out with WD-40 or a solvent. Before immersing the motor into any liquid, make sure that there aren't any parts that may be harmed. One common example is the sparking wheel on some Marx ratchet motors; soaking them in liquid may ruin them. The motor should be inspected for any gummed up oil that didn't get cleaned out. A Q-tip or paint brush soaked in solvent may be used to scrub it out. Finally, blow the motor out with compressed air to remove any remaining solvent.

Once the motor is clean, I like to lubricate it with Turbine Oil. The brand I use is Norvey, and can be found in hardware stores. It is a lightweight, non-gumming oil intended for use in fan motors and other applications that see a lot of operation with intermittent lubrication. An alternative is a good brand of synthetic motor oil, since they are also resistant to gumming up. Don't rely on WD-40 for lubrication... it is useful for cleaning, but it isn't a good long term lubricant. I keep a small bottle of turbine oil handy, and use a small length of wire to apply it. Dip the wire in the oil, then touch the end of it to the point that you want to lubricate. Make sure you lube all moving points; everywhere a shaft rotates in the sideplates, axles, and even wheels if they are able to spin independent of the axle. Don't forget to lubricate the moving parts of the ratchet. The mainspring may be left dry or lubricated; there are specialty lubricants that are available for mainsprings, but I have had good results with turbine oil. It is usually best to keep the oil out of the governor; specifics will be discussed in the "Governors" section. After lubrication, I like to wind the motor up and let it run down while holding it; I watch the motor run and make sure that no moving points were missed. After running, wipe off any excess oil that may be on the motor. If the motor is running properly, it should be ready for service. If it isn't running, then we will have to determine what is wrong and repair it.

A small bottle of oil and a short length of baling wire.

The end of the wire is dipped in the oil, then touched to the point that needs lubrication.

CHAPTER 3
MAINSPRINGS

Next to cleaning and lubrication, a broken mainspring is one of the most common windup motor problems. Broken mainsprings can happen to any windup motor. While careful winding and use will minimize mainspring failures, we have to realize that when a mainspring is wound up, it is put under stress and its shape is distorted. As it unwinds, it returns to its normal state and is under a minimum amount of stress. Even quality spring steel can only take so many of these windup and wind down cycles before the metal becomes fatigued and breaks. When we consider the fact that these trains are many decades old, it should come as no surprise that we will need to learn how to deal with broken mainsprings.

Precautions – Always wear eye protection and heavy leather gloves when working with mainsprings. Even when unwound, the springs are usually constrained somewhat inside the motor. There will be energy released when they are removed, and that energy can cause them to whip around suddenly and with a surprising amount of force. A broken mainspring will have a sharp, jagged edge at the break which is very effective at cutting skin. Even the normal outside end of a mainspring can cause damage. SAFETY FIRST!

Removal – Most mainsprings may be removed without disassembling the motor. This should be done with the spring unwound. Normally, this can be done with a vice to hold the motor, some flat blade screwdrivers (for prying) and some different styles of pliers, such as needle nose, slip-joint and locking pliers. Here are some tips for taking the mainspring out of some common brands of motors.

Marx: For most motors, the mainspring's outside end hooks on a tab that is part of a crossmember between the sideplates. I like to carefully clamp the motor in a vice – making sure that the vice is squeezing on the ends of the crossmembers (NOT the sideplates) – and then use flat blade screwdrivers to carefully unhook the spring from the tab. This may take more force than you would expect, especially with a broken mainspring that has unwound rapidly and jammed itself against the crossmember. Work carefully and patiently. You will probably have to pry the spring slightly away from the tab to get it to move one way or the other. Some oil will help it slide past crossmembers and shafts. Once it is unhooked, grab the end with a pair of pliers to start pulling it out of the motor. One tip: The loose tail of a mainspring can whip around unexpectedly and hurt you, but you can feed it down a length of pipe to keep it under control. Once you get used to removing the springs, you will be able to do it safely without the pipe if you wish. With the outside part of the broken mainspring removed, you will need to take pliers and carefully unwind the broken tail from the mainspring hub. A Marx mainspring has a slightly narrowed end that slides through a slot in the hub. These can be a bit cantankerous to remove, so be patient and methodical.

Marx mainsprings may be removed without any motor disassembly. However, it is easier for the novice if the wheels are removed and the motor is clamped in a vice, so the following steps are shown using this technique. However, if you prefer, this may be done without pulling the wheels or using a vice. Make sure you wear eye protection and leather gloves!

Unhooking a Marx mainspring for removal:

Step 1: With the motor clamped in a vice across the ends of the lower crossmember, the end of the mainspring is forced inward with a screwdriver to release the spring from the tab.

Step 2: The end of the spring is pushed up using the first screwdriver, and a small screwdriver is inserted into the hole in the end of the mainspring.

Step 3: Use the small screwdriver to carefully pry the end of the mainspring upward from in between the crossmember and inside coils of the spring. Be careful to stay out of the way of the spring when it comes loose from the motor.

Step 4: Use a pair of locking pliers to grab the end of the mainspring, then gently pull the spring out of the motor. The drive axle may spin as the spring is removed.

Below: A Marx mainspring and hub from a Ratchet Motor. The inside end of the mainspring is partially removed to show how the spring is inserted into the slot in the hub.

Ives: The Ives mainsprings are usually hooked over a round crossmember. If you are lucky, there will just be a U-shaped hook bent into the outside end of the mainspring that you can simply pull off the crossmember. However, some Ives mainsprings have a complete loop end; the end is formed into a loop and riveted back onto itself. If you are dealing with a loop end, you have a couple of options. One is to remove the crossmember. This is done by center punching the ends, then carefully drilling them out with a small drill bit (see pages 24-28). You want to make sure that you don't use too big of a bit, or get too far off center, otherwise you might mess up the hole in the sideplate. Once you have drilled out both ends, use pliers to grab the crossmember with a slight twisting motion to break it loose. A new crossmember may be machined and swaged back into place, or you could use a threaded standoff of the proper length (like those used to hold electronic boards to the enclosure) and bolt it in with machine screws. Another option is to try to cut the mainspring or drill out the rivet on the loop end. Although mainsprings are tempered and difficult to cut in the middle area, they are usually annealed at the ends. A good pair of diagonal cutters might be sufficient to cut the loop, or careful use of a Dremel tool would do the trick. Be aware that when the spring is cut, the end WILL fly out a little ways – be careful! Once the end is loose, just use pliers to pull it out of the motor, similar to a Marx spring. The inside end will have a small hole on it that engages a catch on the mainspring hub. Unwind the tail and it should unhook from the catch.

Below: A loop end termination on an Ives mainspring.

Hafner: It is my opinion that Hafner mainsprings are the most difficult to remove. Whereas most brands wind up the mainspring by rotating the mainspring hub with the key, Hafner (and early AF motors designed by Hafner) have the mainspring encased in a basket, and the key rotates the basket to wind the mainspring from the outside. This rotating basket makes removing and installing the mainspring a challenge. In order to unhook the mainspring from the basket, the motor has to be completely disassembled. However, there is a way around that, but it isn't pretty. The outer termination has to be cut in order to free the end of the mainspring (unless you want to disassemble the motor… and you don't want to disassemble a Hafner… more on that later). Once the end of the mainspring is cut loose, it is almost guaranteed that you won't be able to pull it out like other brands – it will be bound up too tightly against the fingers of the basket. This means you need to carefully work the spring out from underneath the fingers – one by one – slipping it in between the end of the finger and the brass big gear. The big gear will have to move somewhat to make this happen – remember, I said this wasn't pretty – so you have to be very careful or you risk damaging the gear. Once you have relieved enough tension by working the spring out from under several fingers, you will be able to pull it out with pliers just like the others. The inside tail of the spring has a hole in it that hooks on a catch on the mainspring hub, so unwind it and it will pull off, although the fingers of the mainspring basket make this a real challenge. If you are lucky, the mainspring will be broken. If you aren't lucky… well, it will be time to do some machine work. More on that later.

Below: A factory Hafner mainspring termination. The spring has a tab that engages a slot in one finger of the basket. In order to remove the mainspring without cutting it, the motor would have to be completely disassembled so the mainspring could be rotated about 30 degrees to allow the tab to pass through the slot. It is much easier to cut the mainspring where it narrows down to fit in the slot using a large pair of diagonal cutters.

Above: If the mainspring is bound up too tight against the basket fingers and cannot be pulled out with pliers, it will be necessary to carefully work it out sideways in between the gap between each finger and the big gear. The end of the pencil is pointing at this small gap.

Below: A re-terminated Hafner mainspring. After cutting the mainspring and removing it, the end is ground down so it is narrow enough to fit through the end of the slot. It is then heated to a bright red and carefully formed into a hook. This allows the spring to be connected or disconnected from the slot at any time without further modification.

Removing the mainspring from other brands of motors will usually be similar to the three brands we discussed. So once the mainspring is out, it is time to make a decision – Repair or Replace?

If the break in the mainspring is close to one of the ends, it may be possible to repair the mainspring by re-terminating it. However, if the break is in the middle, the spring may be too short to reuse. A shorter mainspring will reduce the run time. In that case, it is best to use a different spring. It may be possible to find a donor motor with a good mainspring, or you might be able to find a usable mainspring from a place that sells parts for repairing clocks. The critical dimensions of the mainspring are the length, width and thickness. The length may be measured by clamping one end of the spring in a vice and carefully stretching it out so it can be measured. Remember to wear gloves and use eye protection. It is easier if you can recruit a person to help; one to stretch the spring, the other to measure. If the spring is broken, measure both pieces of the mainspring and add them together. A slightly shorter or longer spring is OK. Don't get the idea that a much longer spring will increase runtime, though – the length of the spring has to be balanced against the room it has to expand and contract, so after a point, a longer spring can actually start to reduce the running distance. The width is easy to measure, and this is usually the easiest spec to match. The thickness will have to be measured with calipers or a micrometer. A thicker mainspring will store more power than a thinner one. If the motor had sufficient power with the original spring, there is no need to install a thicker mainspring. The usual problem is that it can be difficult to find a replacement clock mainspring that is as thick as the original. A thinner spring will probably work, although the loss of power might be a problem. There is a good possibility that one or both of the ends on the new mainspring will be different than the old spring, which brings us to the next subject:

Termination – This is the process of modifying the end of the mainspring so it will connect properly to the motor. If you are repairing a broken mainspring, you need to alter the broken end so it matches the original termination. If you are replacing the mainspring, you will need to make sure that both ends of the new spring match the respective ends of the old one. There are three types of ends that are normally used: Loop/Hook end, Hole end or Tab end. The spring will need to be annealed, then bent, drilled or ground to the proper shape.

Annealing: This is the process of using a propane torch to heat the end of the spring to a cherry red color, then letting it cool down slowly. This makes the end of the spring softer so it can be drilled or ground easily. It also removes the springiness from the spring. I like to clamp the spring in a vice during the process. When annealing the inside end of the spring, it is good practice to go back far enough for the annealed part of the spring to make a full wrap around the mainspring hub. This will minimize the chance of the end breaking again. It is also good practice to anneal the outer end a little further than absolutely necessary for the same reason… an extra inch or so should work.

Making a Loop or hook: In practice, this is the same procedure. A true looped mainspring that is riveted back to itself isn't usually needed. A long hook will work fine. Heat the spring up to a cherry red, then quickly form it around a bolt of the proper size. Don't be afraid to do it in multiple steps as needed; heat, form, heat, form. Don't bend it when it is cold… work it while it is hot to minimize the chance of breakage. Remember to let it cool down naturally, do not quench it in water or oil!

Making a hole: Once you have annealed the end of the spring, you should be able to mark the spot for the hole, dimple it with a center punch, and then drill it. Use the smallest hole that will go over the catch, so the end will have maximum strength. Carefully remove the burrs from the edge of the hole, using a chamfer tool or a somewhat larger drill bit.

Making a Tab: Some trains use a tab to terminate the mainspring. For instance, a typical Marx mainspring has a narrow section on the inside end that fits into a slot in the mainspring hub. This can be ground to shape with a bench grinder. Grinding may be done before or after annealing, but I prefer to anneal it first. Other brands, such as Joy Line and Hafner, use a tab on the outside end, which may be formed by grinding a narrow spot by the end of the spring. If it will work, I prefer to just grind a narrow tail on the end and form it into a hook shape instead of going to the trouble of grinding the original tab shape.

Above: Annealing the broken end of a mainspring.

Below: Using a bench grinder to square up the end of a broken mainspring. It can also be used to grind the end of the spring to whatever shape might be needed to terminate it.

Above: A tab end termination (left) and a hole end termination (right). Even though the right spring has an oval shaped hole, a normal drilled round hole will work just fine. However, it may be a bit more difficult to hook it on the catch.

Once the ends are properly terminated, it is time to put the mainspring in the motor.

Installation – With most brands of trains, installation is as simple as hooking the mainspring to the hub, then winding it in with the key, and finally hooking the outside end to the crossmember. Astute readers will note that I said simple… not easy. It can be quite a challenge to get the mainspring connected to the hub. After all, the hub is buried down inside a narrow motor, with only limited access. Using screwdrivers, pliers and a lot of patience, it can be done. First, check and double-check that you are installing the mainspring in the right direction! It is very frustrating to go to the trouble of connecting the mainspring to the hub, just to discover that you hooked it up backward. When you are sure of the direction, it is time to connect the spring to the hub. Most brands will just need the catch to grab the hole in the end of the spring, but Marx requires inserting the narrow section into the slot. Note that the slot does not go through the center of the hub, it is off center. By looking carefully at the slot, you should be able to see how inserting it one way will make the end bend a small amount, and inserting it on the opposite side of the hub will make it bend further. We want to insert it so it does a minimum amount of bending.

Once the inside end is connected to the mainspring hub, use the key to wind it into place. Again, remember to use eye protection and wear leather gloves. It is possible that the new termination could break, and we don't want to get hurt if it does. Watch the tail of the spring as you are winding it in; use the pipe trick to control it if needed. When the mainspring is mostly wound into place, use pliers and screwdrivers to guide the outer end to connect it to the crossmember. At this point, the motor should wind up and run. Be careful when winding it for the first couple of times; keep the leather gloves and eye protection on!

For a Hafner motor, the installation procedure is a bit more complicated. Connecting the mainspring to the catch is similar to other brands, although the fingers of the basket make it a bit more difficult. It is important to make sure the mainspring is coming out of the basket on the proper side of the finger with the termination before winding it in. Once the spring is connected to the hub, it has to be wound in by rotating the drive wheels backward. I like to use a wood match inserted in the spokes. It is a slow process, but it does work. Connecting the outer end of the mainspring to the basket is straightforward, but needs to be done carefully. It is easier to clamp the motor in a vice, which leaves one hand free to wind the drive wheels, and the other hand to hold the needle nose pliers used to hook the spring in the slot.

Above: Using a matchstick to wind a Hafner mainspring into the motor by turning the drive wheels backward.

Now that we know how to replace a mainspring, let's look at some guidelines that will help us get the longest life out of those springs. Don't wind up a cold mainspring; if the locomotive has been stored in cold temperatures, give it a chance to warm up to ambient temperature before winding. Although it doesn't hurt a mainspring to wind it all the way to spring bind, trying to wind it any further will put extra stress on the spring. It is best to know how many turns to wind the springs in your trains so you don't constantly stress the spring by abruptly hitting the binding point. After running the trains, always pick them up and let the spring run down all the way. Leaving a spring wound – especially fully wound – may diminish its power over time. Of course, we want to avoid any rust on the mainspring, so be careful where the trains are stored.

One final note: When a windup train comes to a normal stop, there will still be a small amount of energy left in the mainspring. Pick it up, and you will see the wheels spin for a little bit. So, if the train stops at the back of the layout, no harm in taking a stick and gently pushing it around to a point that you can reach it - the mainspring will still have enough tension on it to keep everything in place. However, pushing it a long ways may cause the inside end of the mainspring to unhook from the hub, or – even worse – fold back around on itself and break at the tight bend. This sometimes happened when little kids got tired of winding up their trains. They would push it around all afternoon, and then when they went to wind it up again, it was broken. So, don't be afraid to move the train a little ways, just don't overdo it.

CHAPTER 4
MOTOR DISASSEMBLY

If the motor has internal mechanical problems, it is likely that it will have to be disassembled for repair. This isn't very straightforward, since most domestic windup trains were built as toys that were meant to be used until they broke, then discarded instead of being repaired. With this in mind, manufacturers built the motors by swaging the crossmembers and motor sideplates together – no thought was given to future disassembly. Fortunately, there are ways to get them apart, although some are easier to work on than others.

Even if you are able to take a motor completely apart, it is rarely necessary. Oftentimes it is possible to replace broken parts with only partial disassembly of the motor. I feel it is best to disturb the motor as little as possible. With that in mind, let's take a look at disassembly techniques for Marx, Ives and Hafner.

Marx (Ratchet Motor): This is one of the easier brands to disassemble. The first thing you may need to do is remove the wheels. Marx wheels are pressed on the axles, so you will need a wheel puller to take them off. Commercial pullers are available, but I use a modified faucet handle puller from the hardware store as shown on page 20. Depending on what is wrong with the motor, you might not have to pull all four wheels. In a ratchet motor, the mainspring hub, ratchet and intermediate gear sets can be accessed without pulling the front wheels. The governor can be removed without pulling any wheels. But, if the drive axle gear set has to be replaced, the entire motor will have to be disassembled.

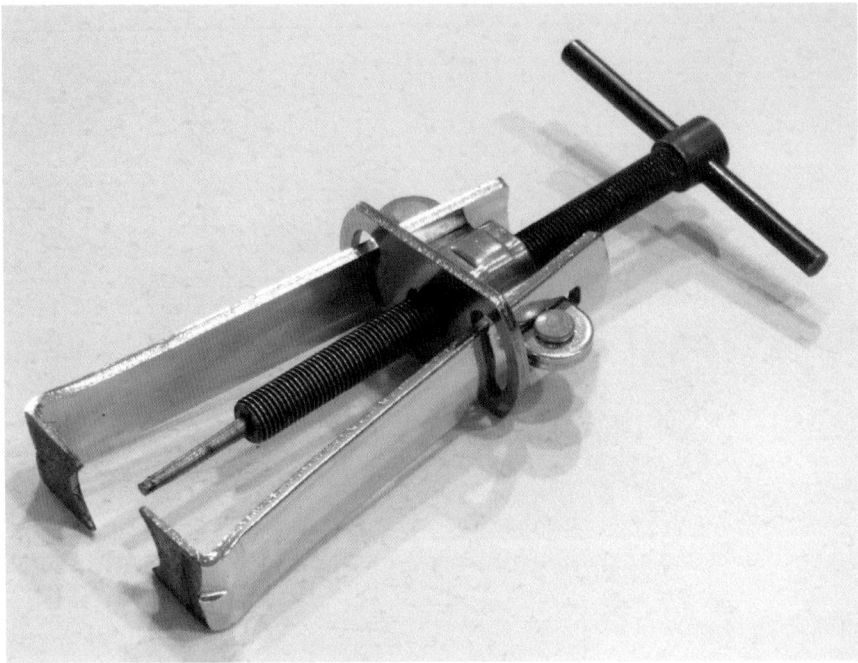

Above: A modified faucet handle puller. The ears that fit under the wheels have been ground so they are thin enough to fit between the motor and wheel.

Below: Pulling a wheel with the puller. The round part that pushes against the end of the axle may have to be ground down so it will fit through the axle hole in the wheel.

Once you have removed the wheels that are in the way, you need to unhook and pull some of the mainspring out of the motor. As the mainspring unwinds, it is actually under compression in the motor. If you disassemble the motor without reducing this stress, it can fly apart and hurt you. The mainspring doesn't have to come all the way out; just unhook the end and pull enough out until the stress in the spring is minimized.

Now it is time to actually start separating the sideplates from the crossmembers. Using a large set of locking pliers, lock them on one of the crossmembers, just about 1/16" from the right sideplate. Insert a large flat blade screwdriver between the plier jaws and the sideplate, then carefully twist to force the sideplate off the crossmember. Work the blade around to minimize the bending of the sideplate – although some bending is unavoidable. You will need to straighten it out with pliers before reassembly. Using two screwdrivers - one on either side of the crossmember – can help minimize damage to the sideplate. Separate only the crossmembers that are absolutely necessary. To remove the mainspring hub, ratchet or intermediate shafts, separate the right sideplate from the two rear crossmembers. The front bottom crossmember is the only one that has to come loose for the governor.

Most Marx windup motors will also have an additional front crossmember that functions as the front motor mount, and guides the siderods on the steam locomotives. It is held in place by two tabs that are slightly twisted. The tabs can be carefully straightened in order to remove the crossmember/motor mount.

Below: Using needle nose pliers to straighten the tabs that hold the front crossmember/motor mount in place.

Above: How to position the locking pliers and flat blade screwdrivers to separate the sideplate from the bottom rear crossmember on a Marx Ratchet Motor.

Below: Even with careful removal, the corner of the sideplate will probably be bent a little. It will need to be straightened before reassembly.

Above: Once the sideplate is separated from both of the rear crossmembers, it may be gently pried out far enough to remove the mainspring/ratchet assembly and intermediate shafts.

Below: Straightening a bent corner on the sideplate using needle nose pliers:

If the motor has to come completely apart, it will be necessary to separate the sideplates from the bell stud. The bell stud is more difficult to remove from the sideplate than the other crossmembers. As the name implies, this particular part is round, and holds the bell (on motors that have a bell) and also holds a gearset for the sparker (on motors that have a sparker). For whatever reason, this stud seems to be swaged much more securely than the flat crossmembers. To complicate matters, the bell and gears make it impossible to use the locking pliers & screwdriver technique that is used on the flat crossmembers. So, the only thing left to do is use a center punch to make a dimple in the middle of each end of the bell stud, then use a small drill to carefully drill it out. Don't use too big of a drill bit or there is a risk of damaging the sideplates. The downside to this is that a new stud will need to be machined in order to reassemble the motor. It isn't a difficult job if you have a metal lathe, but next to impossible if you don't. One option – assuming that you don't require a bell or sparker – is to replace the bell stud with a standoff. I like to buy 3/4" long standoffs that are threaded 4-40 or 6-32 to use as motor crossmembers. It may be necessary to file a little bit off one side so it doesn't hit any gears.

The following pages have a step-by-step pictorial guide to separating the bell stud from the sideplate. The same technique will work for any motor with round crossmembers.

Below: The end of a Marx bell stud protruding through the motor sideplate.

Step 1: Center punch the end of the stud. The X is rarely centered on the stud, so it will be necessary to line up the center punch by eye. Make sure the other end of the stud is backed up by something solid like a vice or anvil.

Step 2: Check your work. The dimple may be moved slightly by punching it again at an angle. It won't hurt anything if the dimple is slightly off center, as long as you are careful when drilling.

Step 3: Drilling out the center. The trick is to use as large of a drill bit as possible without damaging the sideplate. The safe way to do this is to start with a small bit, then re-drill with the next larger bit until the hole in the stud is big enough. I prefer to use a drill press, but this can be done using a hand drill. It is only necessary to drill slightly deeper than the depth of the sideplate.

This is a properly drilled stud:

Step 4: Apply a little pressure to the motor sideplates, forcing them apart. If all goes well, the drilled end of the stud should pull free from the plate.

Step 5: Once the rest of the crossmembers are separated from the sideplate you will be able to remove it entirely. Be ready for everything inside the motor to fall out of place. Sparking motors have a gearset on this shaft that will now slip off the end. Repeat the procedure to remove the bell and stud from the left motor sideplate.

Ives: Again, the first step is wheel removal. The driven wheels are threaded on the axle, so they unscrew in a counter-clockwise direction. It may be necessary to use pliers to hold the axle still. However, the idler wheels are a different story. They are typically held in place by the swaged end of the axle. The axle may be center punched and drilled, or it might be possible to cut it in half with a pair of diagonal cutters. Either way, a new axle will be necessary when the motor is reassembled. A proper replacement will have to be machined on a lathe, but if you don't mind a non-original repair, a straight shaft with spacers behind the wheels will work.

Now for the bad news: If you read through the Marx section, then you know how much trouble it is to separate the sideplates from the bell stud in a Marx ratchet motor. Ives has all round crossmembers... so it is like the entire motor is put together with Marx bell studs. However, it is sometimes possible to clamp locking pliers on the crossmembers and separate them from the sideplates using a flat blade screwdriver. If the crossmembers don't want to come loose, then they will need to be center punched and drilled. My experience has been that they almost always need to be drilled. Again, the crossmembers may be replaced with standoffs of the appropriate length, or new ones machined out of steel. Like the Marx motor, depending on the problem, it may be possible to remove the broken part with only partial disassembly of the motor. However, ratchet problems will most likely require complete disassembly of the motor.

Below: Ives idler wheels from a No. 19 motor. The swaged ends have been drilled out of the old axle so the wheels could be removed and the motor disassembled. A new axle has been machined out of cold rolled steel.

Hafner: The rear idler wheels are swaged on the axle similar to the Ives motors. I usually cut the axle in half to remove them. A new axle can be cut from a length of 0.140" steel rod, and the ends peened over to reassemble everything. Most common problems with a Hafner motor will only require the removal of the rear idler wheels. The driven wheels are also swaged on the axle, but it isn't nearly as easy to replace it. The drive axle not only has a gear fixed to it, but also a square piece behind each wheel to provide a positive drive to the wheel. It's not impossible to replace, but it is very difficult. Don't take it apart unless absolutely necessary.

Early Hafner motors have sections of the left sideplate folded at a 90 degree angle to form the crossmembers. These are attached with small folded tabs to the right sideplate. Those small tabs can be straightened to allow separation of the right sideplate. There are two tips to lessen the chances of breaking off the small tabs. First, don't bend them any further than necessary to remove the sideplate. Second, use a solder gun to apply heat to the bend as you move the tab, both to disassemble and reassemble the motor.

Later Hafner motors use a single sheet metal piece bent in a big "U" shape as the crossmember. Tabs from the center part are swaged into slots in the sideplates. The locking pliers and screwdriver technique can be used to separate the right sideplate from the center piece, starting with the tab closest to the back axle. After separating that tab, move to the next tab away and separate it using just the screwdriver wedged between the center piece and the sideplate, then to the tab at the top of the sideplate. Those are sufficient to remove the mainspring hub and intermediate shafts.

Below: An early Hafner motor on the left, and a later Hafner motor on the right.

CHAPTER 5
GEARS

Stripped gears have to be replaced. For common motors, it is usually best to buy a donor motor for parts. Of course, for common motors, it is probably easier just to buy a running replacement. However, I like to pick up broken motors cheap for parts.

If you have a donor motor, it is easy enough to swap out a complete intermediate shaft and gearset assembly for a good one. Complete disassembly of the motor usually isn't necessary; just pop enough of the crossmembers loose so that the sideplates can be spread far enough apart to get the entire shaft and gearset out. Use needle nose pliers to grab the shaft, and pull the shaft free of the sideplates one end at a time. Carefully work the replacement shaft into the motor the same way.

If you don't have a donor motor or spare parts for a particular brand, you have to get resourceful. Sometimes you can find a workable replacement gear out of a different brand of motor. Another option is to order a new gear from an industrial supply company such as Stock Drive Products. It won't be cheap, and it will take some machining to make it fit, but sometimes it is the only way to get a replacement gear. To order a gear, you will need to know how many teeth it has (easy to count) and the pitch of the gear. The pitch can be estimated by dividing the number of teeth by the diameter of the gear. Measuring the diameter of the gear to the middle of the height of the teeth will be close enough. The last resort would be to make a gear – but describing the process of machining of a gear is beyond the scope of this book.

Above: A stripped gearset from a Marx Ratchet motor.
Note that both the pinion gear and the large gear are damaged.

Below: A replacement gearset for an Ives motor.
Commercially available 48 pitch gears are pressed on a custom machined shaft.

CHAPTER 6
GOVERNORS & ESCAPEMENTS

As was mentioned earlier, windup motors need a mechanism to limit their running speed. Most manufacturers used some type of centrifugal governor, although there are some motors that have a simple escapement.

Centrifugal Governors: This governor typically has a spinning shaft with a weight connected to it. The weight is spring loaded to hold it close to the governor shaft. When the governor spins fast enough that the centrifugal force on the weight is greater than the strength of the spring, the weight will move away from the shaft. The outward movement of the weight will allow it to come into contact with either a stationary drum that surrounds the governor or a nearby crossmember. The contact provides enough friction to limit the speed of the motor. The speed of the motor is determined by three things: the mass of the weight, the strength of the spring, and the gearing between the axle and the governor. Some motors have the governor weights located on the drive axle, typically located behind one of the wheels. Most will have some sort of gearing between the drive axle and the governor, which will allow a smaller governor to limit the motor to a slower speed than otherwise possible. Ives governors are just a spiral spring with a tight coil of wire at the outer end which is usually filled with solder for weight. The weight contacts a crossmember to limit the speed of the motor. A centrifugal governor is a simple mechanism, but it isn't unusual to have problems with them. Since Marx Ratchet and Riser Gear motors use a typical internal centrifugal governor, we will take a look at some common issues that they have.

First, the governor usually needs to be clean and free of oil. If the governor is oily, it can cause the motor to run too fast by reducing the friction between the weight and the drum. A Q-tip can be used to clean out the drum using solvent; while a small piece of paper towel dipped in solvent can be used to clean off the face of the weight where it contacts the drum. On rare occasion, I have seen governors that have the wrong combination of play in the weight and enough friction between the weight and drum to cause them to chatter. The weight flies out, contacts the drum, and there is enough slop between the shaft and the weight that it momentarily stops. The running motor soon takes up the play and makes the weight jump, stop and the process repeats itself… usually in a very rapid fashion. The motor may run in a very erratic or jerky manner. In this case, it is worth trying a small drop of oil in the governor to reduce the friction just a bit. The motor will run smoother, and hopefully it won't run too fast.

The second common issue with a Marx internal governor is the weight itself. They are a die-casting and are subject to zinc pest. In some cases, the weight will disintegrate, causing the rest of the governor to drag or jam up. This is rare, but when it does happen the only options are to machine a new weight or replace the governor with one from a donor motor. Another more common problem is that the weight deforms over time. Usually this happens where the governor touches the shaft, and can cause the end of the small wire that connects the weight to the shaft and spring to drag on the drum at low speeds. Instead of coasting to a gentle stop, the motor will stop somewhat abruptly. It is also possible that the side of the deformed weight may start to drag all the time, causing sluggish operation. In either case, the governor will need to be removed. If the deformation is severe, the weight or governor will need to be replaced. If it is just a slight deformation, the weight can be filed to keep it from dragging. If the connecting wire is touching the drum when stopped, the end may be trimmed a bit to provide clearance.

The final issue typically seen on a Marx governor is a problem with either the connecting wire or spring. Normally, this happens because something has got into them to bend them out of shape, or someone tried to tweak the governor without taking it out of the motor. Again, the governor will need to come out of the motor and the offending parts replaced.

Disassembly and reassembly isn't complicated, but the small size can make it a bit of a challenge. The right sideplate will need to be separated from the front crossmember in order to remove the governor from the motor. Usually, this can be done without removing any drive wheels, but if more clearance is needed feel free to pull one of the front wheels off. I like to use needle nose plier to grab the governor and gently pull it out of the motor. Now the governor itself can be disassembled. The spring is held in place by a tiny washer that is retained by a flattened area on the end of the wire. Needle nose pliers may be used to carefully work the flattened area back to a round shape so that the washer and spring may be removed. The wire can then be straightened so it can slide back and forth properly to allow the weight to work. The weight can also be separated from the shaft and wire at this time, making it easier to file back into shape if needed. If the spring is damaged, I like to replace it with a Kadee #1875 Knuckle Spring that has been cut to the proper length. The #1875 spring is lighter than the stock Marx spring, so the motor runs at a slower speed. Once you are satisfied with the weight, wire and spring, everything may be reassembled and the end of the wire flattened. I generally use needle nose pliers to flatten out the end, although at times I have resorted to swaging it between a punch and a steel block. Make sure that the end of the wire doesn't drag on the hub before permanently reassembling the motor; trim the end of the wire as needed. I keep an old Marx sideplate with a governor hub on the workbench so I can check the governor wire and weight for proper clearance outside of the motor. Don't forget to clean the weight and drum before reassembly. Use the needle nose pliers to gently insert the governor in place, making sure the shaft lines up with the proper holes in the sideplates. Finally the sideplate is forced back onto the crossmember and the end of the crossmember is gently swaged with a ball peen hammer as described in Chapter 10.

Above: A Marx governor with a replacement Kadee #1875 spring.

Below: A Marx governor that is dragging on the drum. The pencil is pointing to the end of the wire that is touching the drum. This will cause the motor to stop abruptly when the motor is winding down. The end of the wire may be trimmed or ground off to get enough clearance. Note the white corrosion on the die cast weight.

Above: A Marx reversing windup motor governor with a replacement steel weight.

Below: A late model Hafner governor.

Ives governors are a bit simpler, but can be difficult to repair. Sometimes the solder that holds the spring to the shaft will break and just needs to be re-soldered. Be very careful not to overheat the spring itself, or it may lose its springiness. The spring can be carefully adjusted using needle nose pliers. However, if the spring is broken or missing, the repairs can be difficult. Unless you can find a donor motor with a good governor – which is unlikely – you will either have to make a new spiral governor spring using music wire, or replace it with another brand of governor. I've had good results retrofitting Ives motors with modified Marx governors.

Above: An Ives governor. The tight coil is filled with solder. When running, it moves outward and contacts the crossmember to limit the motor's speed.

Below: An Ives motor that has a modified Marx governor installed.

Escapement: This is a much simpler version of the timing mechanism used in a clock. An escape wheel is mounted on the drive axle, and a sheet metal piece forms the anchor and pallets. Since the escapement in a windup motor operates much faster than one in a clock, no pendulum or balance wheel is needed. As the escape wheel rotates, the teeth push the entrance pallet up, rotating the anchor so that as the escape wheel continues to rotate, another tooth will strike the escape pallet and move the anchor in the opposite direction back to its starting position. The motor can accelerate up to the point that the power it takes to make the anchor oscillate is greater than the power delivered by the mainspring. Unfortunately, escapements tend to be less effective than centrifugal governors, even when the escapement is in perfect condition.

The two main problems with escapements are wear and adjustment. The pallets – the parts of the sheet metal anchor that are struck by the escape wheel teeth – can get worn. The anchor itself can get bent out of shape. Finally, the anchor oscillates rapidly back and forth, which tends to wear out its bearing holes in the sideplates. Excessive wear in these holes can reduce the effectiveness of the escapement, or even let the anchor fall out of place.

Although it may be possible to bend the anchor a bit to take care of some wear on the pallets, worn holes in the sideplates are much harder to fix. I have repaired them by adapting a shaft to the anchor, then installing matching bushings in the sideplates. It is a lot of trouble, and the result is an escapement that works as good as new… which is to say, not very well. If there is room, it may be possible to retrofit a centrifugal governor to a motor with a worn out escapement.

Below: A disassembled AF motor with an escapement.

Above: A worn out bearing hole for the anchor in an AF motor (left),
and the same hole after being bored and fitted with a bushing (right).

Below: A repaired anchor for the AF motor. The original tabs on the sides of the anchor
have been removed and replaced by a steel shaft which is soldered in place. The brass
spacers will keep the anchor aligned with the escape wheel when the motor is assembled.

Note the wear on the end of the "pallet" on the left side.
The anchor may be adjusted by bending it slightly to compensate for the wear.

CHAPTER 7
RATCHETS

Most windup motors have a ratchet – a mechanism that allows the mainspring to drive the motor in one direction, but disengages from the rest of the drivetrain when the mainspring is being wound in the opposite direction. Hafner motors have a ratchet, but instead of being in the drivetrain, it is located in between the basket and sideplate. Some motors don't have an actual ratchet, but use a gearset in slotted holes to allow the gears to disengage when rotated in one direction and engage when rotating the opposite direction.

Marx Ratchet Motor: Marx actually used three types of ratchets over the years, not including the Riser Gear motor. However, the most common type of Marx ratchet uses a plate with stamped pawls that engage holes in the big gear next to the mainspring. These pawls can get mushroomed on the edge after many years of use. The edge of the pawl can actually form a hook shape and cause the ratchet to lock up. Sometimes the pawls get rounded off, and the ratchet won't hold when the mainspring is wound up. Either way, the pawls will need to be filed back into the correct shape. If the corners of the pawls are rounded off, it may be necessary to use a hammer and punch to force them a bit further out of the plate, then file them back into shape. If the edges of the holes in the big gear are rounded off, the gear may be flipped over. The edges of the holes on the other side will still be square and should properly engage the filed pawls.

Although the pawls are the most common problem with Marx ratchets, there are a couple of other things that can go wrong with them. A small spring is used to hold the ratchet plate in place. If it is damaged, the ratchet won't engage properly. Another issue is the square die-cast retainer that holds the pawl plate in place. The square part that engages the pawl plate may get rounded and start slipping. The only easy repair for either of these problems is to replace them with good parts from a donor motor. I have machined a replacement hub complete with custom ratchet for a Ratchet Motor, but it isn't a project that I would recommend for the novice windup repairman.

Above: A worn pawl (left) and worn edges on the holes in the big gear (right).

Below: A pawl plate after filing the pawls back into shape. A small file is used to square up the vertical face of each pawl. If a hook has formed on the ramp section of the pawl, it should be filed down smooth to match the angle of the ramp.

As a side note, this pawl plate is from the very first Marx ratchet that I repaired. I'm including this picture to show that even though it was crudely done, the repairs were effective and the locomotive is still running to this day. I have done many since then, and with practice the pawl plates that I file these days look much nicer than this one!

Above: A disassembled Marx ratchet.
Left to right: retainer, spring, pawl plate, big gear, and mainspring hub.

Below: An assembled Marx ratchet.

Ives & AF: The ratchets in these motors usually consist of a ratchet wheel that is pressed on the winding stem, and one or more pawls that move on a pivot attached to the big gear. A spring will keep the pawls pressed against the ratchet wheel. Missing or damaged springs can be formed from music wire. Pawls will have to be fabricated out of metal, and the pins that attach them to the big gear will have to be turned on a metal lathe. It is possible to substitute machine screws for the pins, but they will need to be flush with the spring side of the big gear or they will interfere with the movement of the mainspring. I prefer new pins to machine screws, as I feel the pins are stronger and don't wear out as quickly. A worn out ratchet wheel is rare, but if needed this part will have to be fabricated. As mentioned in the section on disassembly, these types of motors will almost always have to be completely disassembled to remove the ratchet/winding stem/mainspring hub assembly.

Below: A damaged Ives ratchet. Although the pawl and ratchet wheel are useable, the pawl spring is broken, the big gear stripped, and the winding stem is rounded off. It is easy enough to make and install a new spring for the pawl, but the big gear and winding stem need to be replaced. In this case, I chose to make an entirely new assembly.

Above: A replacement ratchet assembly for an Ives motor.

The big gear is a commercial 48 pitch brass gear modified to accept the pawl and winding stem. The new winding stem, ratchet wheel, pawl and pin are machined out of cold rolled steel. The pawl spring was formed out of music wire.

CHAPTER 8
MAINSPRING HUBS

Marx and Hafner mainspring hubs are die-cast, and occasionally fail due to zinc pest. Marx hubs are pretty common, and it is easiest to find a donor motor for a replacement. I have machined a replacement Marx hub out of yellow brass, but there usually isn't any need to do that. Hafner mainspring hubs are a different story. It seems like most Hafner donor motors I get have a broken mainspring hub, so I have made quite a few replacements out of yellow brass. The parts need to be machined on a lathe, so it isn't a job for everyone. The catch and shaft are usually undamaged and may be reused. Drill out the big gear to remove the remains of the original hub, then solder the gear to the new hub.

Below: A Hafner mainspring hub that has broken due to zinc pest.

Above: The individual parts needed to repair a Hafner mainspring hub. The big brass gear and small steel shaft/catch are original parts. The two small brass parts replace the broken die-cast piece as seen in the pictures on the previous page. The hub is soldered to the big gear with a good silver bearing solder.

Below: A repaired Hafner mainspring hub assembly.

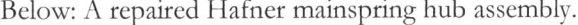

Above: A replacement hub machined out of brass for a Marx Ratchet Motor (left) and the broken original hub (right). The new hub is designed to use a custom ratchet.

Below: A broken hub for a Marx Riser Gear motor (left) and a custom made replacement hub installed in the motor (right).

CHAPTER 9
WORN BEARINGS

Most windup motors use sheet metal for the sideplates. There aren't any actual bearings; the shafts just rotate in holes in the steel sideplates. Surprisingly, wear usually isn't much of a problem. However, there are a couple of exceptions. The first one has already been covered – the holes for the escapement anchor tend to wear quickly. The other exception is the bearing holes for the first intermediate shaft in the motor. This is the shaft that is located closest to the big gear and mainspring. It has a lot of stress on it, and tends to be the same small size as the other intermediate shafts in the motor. Sometimes those holes will be worn into a slot, and can let the pinion gear move away from the big gear resulting in a catastrophic failure.

A worn bearing hole isn't an easy fix. It will likely involve some machining. If the shaft isn't worn out, it is possible to reuse it and fit a bushing in the motor. The sideplate will need to be bored out in a milling machine using an end mill so that the hole is in the right spot. Don't try to simply drill it out, as the center of the resulting hole will be a bit out of place. A new bushing will need to be turned on a lathe. It can be pressed into the sideplate and soldered to help keep it in place. An alternative is to drill the proper size hole in a small piece of sheet metal, and solder it in place on the inside of the motor. This may not be possible if the shaft has a gear next to the worn hole, or if there is interference from another part. Another consideration is that it may be necessary to fabricate spacers to keep the shaft from slipping out the side of the motor, since the journals are usually smaller than the rest of the shaft to keep it in place. A final option is to bore out the bearing holes and then retrofit a larger shaft to the gearset.

Above: Boring out a worn bearing hole using a milling machine.

Below Left: A small bushing that has been turned on a metal lathe.
Below Right: The bushing installed in the motor sideplate.

 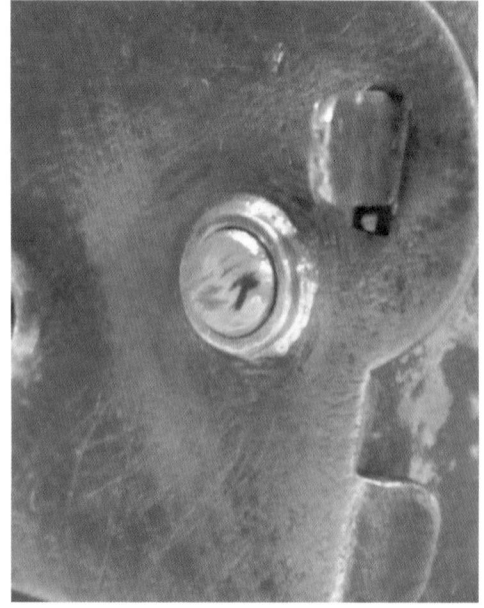

CHAPTER 10
MOTOR REASSEMBLY

Reassembling a windup motor will take some patience. If the motor is to be swaged back together, always do some test fitting before permanently assembling it. Make sure everything lines up and rotates freely before peening the crossmembers. If you have machined new crossmembers, double check that both ends of each crossmember fits properly in their respective motor sideplates, and that they are all the proper length. Take your time – it is very discouraging to get a motor partially reassembled only to find out that the motor has to be taken apart again.

Obviously, new round crossmembers should fit in the sideplates with a minimum of play. I like for them to stick out around 0.030" – 0.040" past the sideplate to allow enough material to peen, but not so much as to be a problem. The Marx flat crossmembers can usually be forced back through the rectangular hole in the sideplate. If it is too tight of a fit, try using a vice to gently push it in place, then use a hammer & punch to finish seating it before it is swaged. On occasion, the Marx crossmembers may have to be filed a bit to let them fit through the sideplate hole without damage. When swaging the Marx crossmembers, the temptation is to peen them over much more than they originally were. Don't do it! Remember that the motor may have to be disassembled again in the future, so don't get carried away with the swaging.

If the motor was taken completely apart – such as an Ives where all the crossmembers had to be replaced – I like to start with the left sideplate and install the crossmembers on it first. Use a piece of steel with a hole drilled in it slightly larger than the small end of the crossmember as a bucking bar. Clamp it in a vice, set the crossmember in the hole, then put the sideplate over the end of the crossmember and peen it over with a small ball-peen hammer. The idea of the bucking bar is that the force is born on the shoulder of the crossmember, not the end. If you simply put the end of the crossmember on a flat surface while swaging the other end, you will probably find that the free end on the surface has mushroomed out enough to keep it from fitting in the sideplate. Make and use the bucking bar to install the crossmembers in the first sideplate… it is worth the trouble.

Above: An Ives motor with all new crossmembers ready for assembly.

Below: An Ives motor ready for the right sideplate to be installed.

Once one sideplate has all the crossmembers attached to it, I like to gently clamp it in a vice, then begin loading up the mainspring hub, intermediate shafts, governor and axles into it. You may want to go ahead and attach the mainspring to the hub while it is out of the motor, since it is much easier to do so than after the motor is assembled. No need to force the entire mainspring into the motor at this point; just set the assembly into place and let the mainspring coils closest to the hub sit inside the motor with the rest of the spring outside. It will be wound into place later.

Now that everything is loaded onto the first sideplate, it is time to start working on setting the second sideplate in place. Be aware that nothing will line up and fall into place. You will need to start from one end, and gently coax everything through its corresponding hole as you work your way to the other end. I like to start at the end with the mainspring hub, guide the ends of it into place and set the sideplate onto the crossmembers at that end of the motor. Don't worry about swaging them yet; use a small C-clamp on the ends of a crossmember to keep it in place. Work your way toward the other end of the motor, using small screwdrivers and needle nose pliers to gently line up the ends of the various shafts into place. It may take a few tries before everything lines up, but be patient. When all the shafts are lined up, slip the sideplate over the remaining crossmembers. Use another small C-clamp to hold it in place. Spin the drive axle to make sure nothing is binding or dragging.

Now you can swage the rest of the ends of the crossmembers. Peen one into place, then spin the motor, peen another, spin and so on. If the motor starts dragging, check to see what is happening before continuing. Once everything is firmly in place and the motor still spins, you may wind in the mainspring. At this point, the motor should be trying to run as you get tension on the spring. Once the mainspring is wound in place and the outer end hooked up, the motor should wind and run normally.

Below: Swaged crossmembers on an Ives motor.

Above: A swaged crossmember on a Marx motor.

The wheels may now be installed. Marx wheels need to be pressed in place using a vice, drill press or arbor press. Flat pieces of steel may be used to help keep them square, and sometimes sockets may be used as well. The wheels usually need to be pressed in a little beyond the end of the axle; if you just press them even with the axle ends the gauge may be too wide. Check the gauge using a section of track and press the wheels in further as needed. Ives and some AF drive wheels simply thread onto the axle – make sure they are snug, but resist the urge to overtighten them. The rear wheels on Ives, Hafner and some other brands have to be placed on the axle, and the axle end swaged to keep them in place. This is delicate work. Make a small bucking bar with a slight dimple drilled in one end that can be clamped in the vice. Place one end of the axle in the dimple, then concentrate on peening the other end without the lower end getting out of place. Gently work around the outer edge of the end of the axle with the peen end of the hammer. If the wheel has siderods, work opposite of the rod, and turn the axle around to the proper position as needed. Work slowly and methodically. It helps to imagine the end of the axle as if it were made out of clay, and visualize how each blow of the hammer displaces the material outward to form the mushroom shape on the axle's end. Give the wheel an occasional pull to see if the swaging is sufficient to keep it in place. Always check the gauge of the wheels on a section of track before swaging and after everything is assembled.

Once the motor is reassembled, oil it as discussed earlier. If you have re-terminated the mainspring, make sure to wear gloves when winding it up for the first time. Some motors can do a test run by themselves; others will have to be mounted in the body. Either way, it is time to run the motor on the track!

Pressing wheels on a Marx motor using a vice (above) and a drill press (below).

Above: Hafner wheels and axle ready to be installed. These wheels were worn out, so they were bored on a lathe to accept custom made hubs.

Below: The Hafner wheel installed on the motor. The end of the axle is carefully swaged using a ball peen hammer. Don't forget to install the spacers between the wheels and motor.

CHAPTER 11
LOOSE WHEELS

Sometimes wheels that are pressed onto axles come loose. The Marx stamped steel wheels are notorious for this. If the stamped steel wheels aren't too wallowed out, then they can be fixed using Loctite. Another option is to use JB Weld as a filler in the middle of the wheel, then press it into place. Axles may be "knurled" using a small chisel to make several small raised parallel lines on the end of the axle. This is also useful for die-cast wheels, especially when combined with Loctite. The last option is to make a replacement axle out of a slightly larger size of steel rod.

Some manufacturers such as Hafner use stamped steel idler wheels that rotate freely on the axle. It isn't unusual to find them worn out, which can cause derailment problems when they get too wobbly. These wheels can be repaired by boring them on a lathe and installing hubs. The hubs are turned on a lathe and swaged in place, as seen on the previous page and in the picture below. The hubs can be made from steel or brass.

Above: A stamped steel Marx drive wheel. They are known for their tendency to come loose on the axle. Loctite or JB Weld may be used to hold them on the axle.

Below: An axle that has been "knurled" using a chisel to form raised lines to hold the wheel in place. These may be used by themselves, or combined with JB Weld or Loctite to repair a loose wheel.

CHAPTER 12
KEYS

Missing keys are a common problem. Fortunately, keys can almost always be bought or made. Almost all windup toy train keys are either square or threaded, and both of those types can be either male or female.

Marx used two kinds of keys; a male threaded key or a square key, with the latter being the most common. Reproduction Marx keys can be purchased from Grossman's Train Parts. The square Marx keys can be formed out of 1/8" key stock from a hardware store.

Many brands have a square winding stem that requires a key with a matching square hole. They can be bought from any clock repair business, although it will be necessary to measure across the flats and convert the measurement to millimeters in order to get the proper size of key.

Some motors need a male or female threaded key. To make a key for these motors, first determine the thread used on the motor. I like to use a machine screw or nut of a known size for this. Chuck up a short length of ¼" steel rod in the lathe and drill a hole in the center of one end. Tap the hole to match the motor. If the motor needs a male key, insert a machine screw – using Loctite – into the rod until it tightens up. Then cut it off to the desired length and dress the threads with a file. Cut a slot in the other end of the rod. A handle can be cut out of 16 gauge steel and filed to the final shape. Insert the handle into the slot in the rod, and solder it in place. For extra strength, it can be cross drilled and pinned. An alternative to the flat steel handle is a length of steel rod welded to the shaft at a 90 degree angle.

Above: Two examples of homemade keys. The left key is a male threaded key using 16 gauge sheet metal for the handle wedged in a slot in the shaft. The handle has been soldered and pinned. The right key is a female threaded key made using ¼" round steel. The handle is a length of steel rod welded to the shaft at a 90 degree angle.

Below: Original male and female threaded keys for American Flyer.

Above: Keys for a square winding stem.
A vintage key is shown on the left, while a modern clock key is shown on the right.

Below: Marx square keys.
On the left is an original Marx key, the one on the right is a modern reproduction.

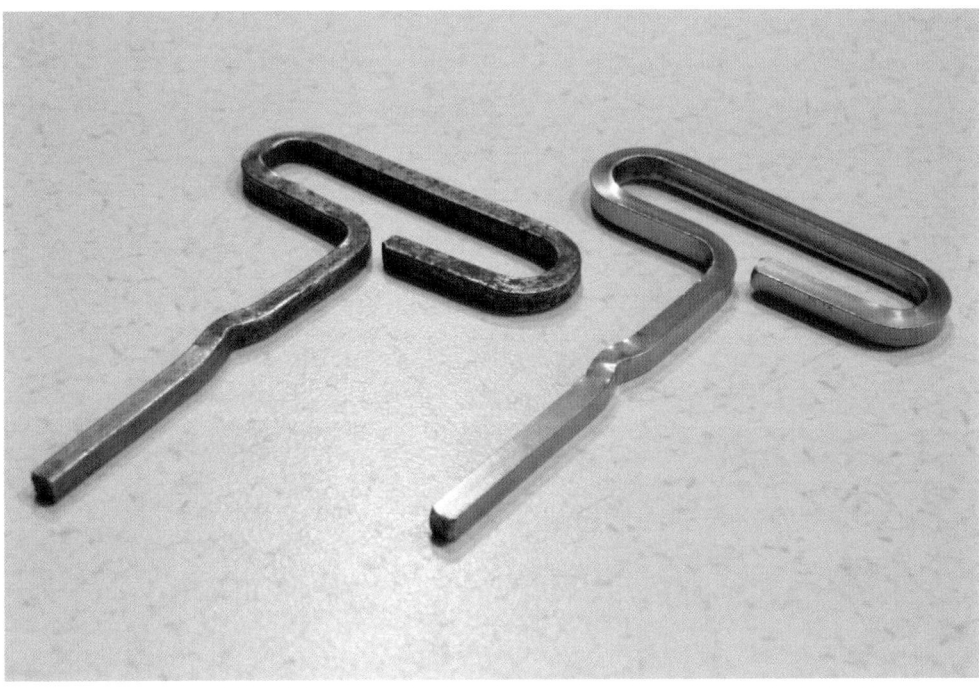

CHAPTER 13
TRAIN CARS

Sometimes, the problem with a windup locomotive isn't the motor itself, but the cars it is trying to pull. Remember that these motors only have a limited amount of power, so it doesn't take much drag to make a drastic change in their performance.

The cars should roll smoothly and with a minimum of drag. On Marx and similar cars, oil the axles where they pass through the body as well as where they pass through the metal wheels. I do not oil the plastic wheels on later Marx cars. Some brands of cars will have the axle fixed solid to the body, in which case you should only oil the wheels, while others may have the wheels fixed solid to the axle requiring oil only at the body.

If the car still drags even though it is oiled, make sure that the body or chassis isn't bent so as to drag on the wheels. Straighten as needed with pliers. It may not be readily apparent, but most manufacturers had either a slight shoulder formed on the outside of the wheel, or a dimple embossed on the inside of the chassis to keep the contact area between the wheel and chassis to a minimum. It only takes a little pressure to bend things out of whack, causing too much contact (and drag) on the wheels. Be sure to roll the car through curves, backward and forward, left and right. Sometimes, the shifting of the car body in the curve will cause drag even though the car rolls freely on the straights.

One last thing to check is the wheels themselves. It isn't unusual to find wheels swapped on old cars, and on occasion I have found a larger wheel from another manufacturer that is dragging the flange on the bottom of the floor of the car. It might spin freely when you pick it up, so look for marks on the underside of the car, and replace the wheels as needed.

Above: A Marx car (left) and an Ives car (right).
The wheel and frame should only touch at the area immediately around the axle.
Below Left: A Marx wheel just barely touching the frame at the center of the wheel.
Below Right: The embossed axle hole on a Marx frame.

CHAPTER 14
THE IVES NO. 19 PROJECT

Some of the pictures that I have used in this book are from an Ives No. 19 that needed a lot of work. The project began as a challenge from my friend Steve. He had a nice Ives No. 19 that happened to be missing a lot of motor parts. The goal of the project was to get the locomotive running without making any visible modifications to the outside of the motor. Also, since the No. 19 is a heavy cast iron locomotive with a high center of gravity, it needed to run at a relatively slow speed in order to stay on the track.

The motor was missing most of the gears and shafts in the mechanism, as well as the governor and mainspring. The winding stem, ratchet and big gear were in the motor, except that the winding stem was rounded off, the pawl spring was broken and the big gear stripped (a picture of the mess is on page 42). As it turned out, the only parts of the motor I was able to use were the sideplates, drive axle, and wheels.

The first step in the process was to disassemble the motor. Since it is an Ives, all the crossmembers had to be drilled out and removed from both sideplates. The drive wheels were unscrewed from the front axle, and the rear axle was drilled out to remove the back wheels. Once the motor was apart, the sideplates were thoroughly cleaned.

Now the hard part began. In order to keep the outside of the motor looking original, I was determined not to drill any new holes. That meant I had to use the existing holes for the various shafts and crossmembers. Using a set of number drills and calipers, I made a diagram of the sideplate with the center-to-center dimensions between all the holes for the shafts, as well as the diameter of each hole. I would find the number drill bit that would just fit in a hole, then find another drill bit to fit in the next hole, measure the distance between them, then add half of the diameter of each bit to get an accurate center-to-center distance.

Now that I had accurate measurements of the bearing holes, I had to figure out what gears I needed. The drive axle had a 48 pitch gear on it, so I decided to use 48 pitch gears throughout the motor. Although the process involved a bit of trial and error, a simple Excel spreadsheet made the calculations go quickly. I would simply choose the number of teeth that I wanted to use on the first gear and pick the center-to-center distance to the next gear from the diagram of the sideplate. The spreadsheet was set up with the following equation:

$$(D-(G1/96))x96=G2$$

Where:
D=The center-to-center distance between the two gears in inches.
G1=The number of teeth on the first gear.
G2=The number of teeth on the second gear.

Ideally, the number of teeth given for G2 would be a whole number, since a gear can't have a fraction of a tooth on it! However, G2 would normally have a few numbers after the decimal point. Usually it wasn't a problem to just drop everything behind the decimal point to round the number down. It is not a good idea to round up unless the amount is very small, since that could make the gears bind up due to a lack of clearance.

The next step is to look through the catalog of gears that your chosen manufacturer offers. For instance, let's say that the center-to-center distance (D) is 1.562" and we want to use a 14 tooth gear for G1. The equation (1.562-(14/96))x96 = 135.952 teeth. In this case, a 135 or 136 tooth gear would probably work just fine, but it isn't guaranteed that the manufacturer offers this size. Let's say that the manufacture only offers a 125 tooth gear. We would need to work the equation again, coming up with a mating gear with 24.952 teeth. If the manufacturer offers a 24 or 25 tooth gear, we are in business. Typically, there are a wider variety of small gears offered, with less choices as the number of teeth increase. This is where the science crosses the line into an art; trying to juggle the available gears to come up with a pair that has the correct center-to-center distance while maintaining an acceptable gear ratio. The goal was to maximize the gear ratio so that the locomotive would run as long as possible. The process was repeated for each set of mating gears. An order was placed, and with the gears in hand I began to machine parts.

Since the entire winding stem, ratchet and big gear assembly had problems, I decided to make a new assembly to replace it. The big gear – like all the replacement gears – was a commercial item, which was modified to work with a custom made winding stem and ratchet. The finished piece (as seen on page 43) was tested in the motor, using blocks of steel as temporary spacers between the sideplates. Once it was spinning freely, the first intermediate shaft was machined and the gears pressed in place. After each new shaft was machined, the motor would be assembled to determine if everything would turn without dragging or binding. Even though the original gear on the drive axle was in good condition and nominally 48 pitch, it still needed a bit of filing and fitting to make it mesh well with the modern gears.

This intermediate shaft had to be designed to hold three gears. The shaft is machined slightly larger than the holes in the gears so they can be pressed into place.

The new gears and shafts are temporarily assembled in the motor
to make sure they spin without any binding or dragging.

There is a very limited amount of room for a governor in an Ives motor. After a couple of attempts, I finally settled on a bevel gear set up so that I could use a large governor in the front of the motor hidden between the cylinders of the body. The governor is a hybrid centrifugal/escapement; it has a spinning weight that is hinged (without any springs) so it will fly out and strike the upper and lower flat areas of the governor housing. It isn't as smooth or quiet as a normal centrifugal governor, but it is effective at limiting the speed of the motor. The governor assembly was painted black to make it less noticeable.

The finished Ives No. 19.

James Pekarek grew up in Ozarks region of southwest Missouri. Even though he pursued a career in electricity and electronics, he was instilled with a fascination for mechanical things early in his childhood. His first trainset was a Marx #526 with a 401 windup locomotive, which is still running despite being well used & abused. He grew up watching his dad work on hit-n-miss engines, tractors, trucks, cars and anything else that needed to be repaired. When he was a teenager, he talked his dad into building a 12" gauge "diesel" locomotive powered by a Briggs & Stratton engine. That was the start of what eventually became the Northview & Frisco Railroad, which now includes a number of "diesel" and live steam locomotives. James still lives in southwest Missouri with his wife Karin. They have a few acres of hilly, wooded land that is home to the 12" gauge N&F Railroad, as well as a dining room full of O gauge windup trains.